WACKY COMPARISONS
HOW TALL?

by Mark Weakland   illustrated by Igor Sinkovec

Wacky Ways to COMPARE HEIGHT

How tall is a PENGUIN?

How tall is a SKUNK?

Is either as tall as a TREE or CHIPMUNK?

A GIRAFFE, a DINO, a SOCCER BALL—

Time to discover how short and how tall!

PICTURE WINDOW BOOKS
a capstone imprint

21 SKUNKS, with a little luck,
stand as tall as
1 GARBAGE TRUCK.

An **NBA PLAYER** with a basketball

is almost as tall as

7 STYLISH DOLLS.

1 player = 6 ft. 8 in. (2 m); 1 doll = 1 ft. (30 cm)

470 CHATTERING CHIPMUNKS can be

as tall as

1 TOWERING REDWOOD TREE.

6

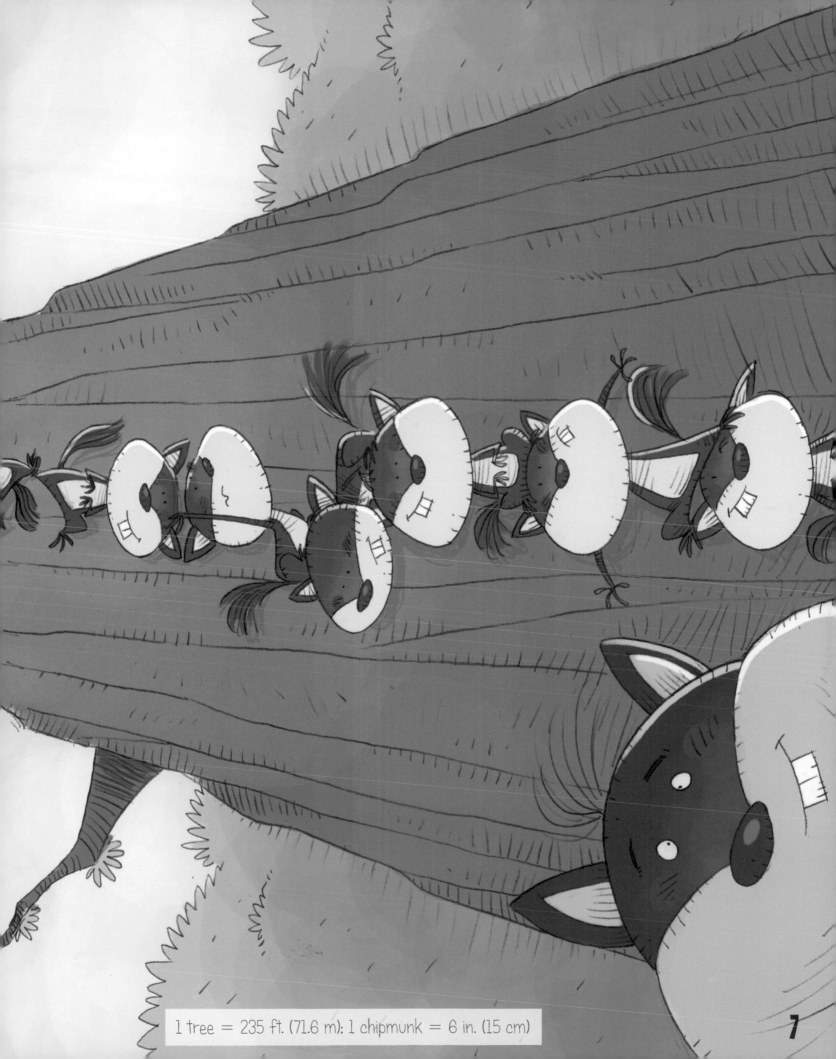

1 tree = 235 ft. (71.6 m); 1 chipmunk = 6 in. (15 cm)

To see to the top, we crane our necks.

36 HOT DOGS equal 1 T. REX!

1 T. rex = 18 ft. (5.5 m); 1 hot dog = 6 in. (15 cm)

9

"The STATUE OF LIBERTY is tall. It's true!"

say 431 PIGEONS who wobble and coo.

1 statue = 305 ft. (93 m); 1 pigeon = 8½ in. (22 cm)

The GREAT PYRAMID has a height a bit greater than **84** REFRIGERATORS.

1 pyramid = 450 ft. (137 m); 1 fridge = 5 ft.. 4 in. (1.6 m)

14 TEDDY BEARS

stand tall and laugh.

BEARS

1 giraffe = 17 ft. (5.2 m); 1 bear = 1 ft., 3 in. (38 cm)

15

1 OSTRICH, feathered and tall,

nearly equals the height of **11** SOCCER BALLS.

1 ostrich = 8 ft. (2.4 m); 1 ball = 9 in. (23 cm)

An **ELEPHANT**,

from bottom to top,

is as tall as **4 FIRE HYDRANTS** that just won't stop!

1 elephant = 10 ft., 6 in. (3.2 m); 1 hydrant = 2 ft., 8 in. (81 cm)

The world's tallest mountain is

MOUNT EVEREST.

How many ELEPHANTS match

its snowy crest?

2,765

1 mountain = 29,035 ft. (8.8 kilometers): 1 elephant = 10 ft. 6 in. (3.2 m)

How many **POPSICLES** should you buy

to match the height of a **BIRD** that can't fly?

READ MORE

Cleary, Brian P. *How Long or How Wide?: A Measuring Guide*. Math Is Categorical. Minneapolis: Millbrook Press, 2007.

Hillman, Ben. *How Big Is It?: A Big Book All About BIGness*. What's the Big Idea? New York: Scholastic Reference, 2007.

Parker, Vic. *How Tall Is Tall?: Comparing Structures*. Measuring and Comparing. Chicago: Heinemann Library, 2011.

INTERNET SITES

FactHound offers a safe, fun way to find Internet sites related to this book. All of the sites on FactHound have been researched by our staff.

Here's all you do:

Visit *www.facthound.com*

Type in this code: 9781404883239

Check out projects, games and lots more at
www.capstonekids.com

Special thanks to our adviser, Terry Flaherty, PhD, Professor of English, Minnesota State University, Mankato, for his expertise.

Editor: Jill Kalz
Designer: Ashlee Suker
Art Director: Nathan Gassman
Production Specialist: Eric Manske
The illustrations in this book were created digitally.

Picture Window Books are published by Capstone,
1710 Roe Crest Drive, North Mankato, Minnesota 56003
www.capstonepub.com

Library of Congress Cataloging-in-Publication Data
Weakland, Mark.
  How tall? : wacky ways to compare height / by Mark Weakland ; illustrated by Igor Sinkovec.
    pages cm. — (Wacky comparisons)
  Summary: "Compares various tall objects to shorter objects in unique, illustrated ways"—Provided by publisher.
  Audience: K to grade 3.
  Includes bibliographical references.
  ISBN 978-1-4048-8323-9 (library binding)
  ISBN 978-1-4795-1913-2 (paperback)
  ISBN 978-1-4795-1909-5 (eBook PDF)
1. Measurement—Juvenile literature. 2. Comparison (Philosophy)—Juvenile literature. I. Sinkovec, Igor, illustrator. II. Title.

QA465.W43 2014
530.8—dc23   2013012150

LOOK FOR ALL THE BOOKS IN THE SERIES:

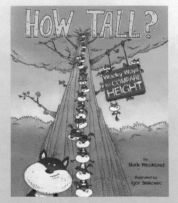

Printed in the United States   6023